BY ORDER OF THE
SECRETARY OF THE AIR FORCE

AIR FORCE CATALOG 21-209V2

2 JUNE 2011
Incorporating Change 1, 19 October 2011

Maintenance

DEMOLITION MUNITIONS

COMPLIANCE WITH THIS PUBLICATION IS MANDATORY

ACCESSIBILITY: Publication and forms are available on the e-Publishing website at http://www.e-publishing.af.mil for downloading or ordering.

RELEASABILITY: There are no releasability restrictions on this publication.

OPR: AFCESA/CEXD

Supersedes: AFCAT21-209V2,
11 January 2005

Certified by: AF/A7CX
(Col Jeffery A. Vinger)
Pages: 44

This Catalog supports Air Force Policy Directive (AFPD) 21-2, *Munitions*. It provides munitions (e.g., blasting caps, demolition blocks, dynamite) authorizations for: training, exercises, evaluations, and competitions; and peacetime emergency response, war and contingency operations, and mobility. It provides guidance to individuals at all levels for estimating, establishing, and changing operational and training munitions authorizations; forecasting correct category codes; and tracking costs, including Air Force Reserve and Air National Guard (ANG) units, except where noted otherwise. Units and command functional areas should continue to use AFCAT 21-209V1 to forecast ground security munitions (e.g., small arms ammunition, grenades, and grenade simulators). Send comments and suggested improvements on AF Form 847, **Recommendation for Change of Publication**, through command channels to AFCESA/CEXD, 139 Barnes Drive, Suite 1, Tyndall AFB FL 32403-5319. Ensure all records created as a result of processes prescribed in this publication are maintained in accordance with Air Force Manual (AFMAN) 33-363, *Management of Records*, and disposed of IAW Air Force Records Information Management System (AFRIMS) Records Disposition Schedule (RDS) located at https://www.my.af.mil/gcss-af61a/afrims/afrims/.

SUMMARY OF CHANGES

This interim change (IC) implements new guidelines for viewing and calculating ground and demolition munitions authorizations via the web based tool.

Chapter 1

GENERAL INFORMATION

1.1. Establishing Munitions Authorizations. Units or functions responsible for an operational mission or training program will send requests to create a munitions authorization to the parent major command (MAJCOM) munitions user functional managers (MUFM). Each request will:

1.1.1. Contain complete explanation of the need for the specific munitions, including how the requirement was calculated (i.e., operational mission [air base defense basic quantity] or training [number of students or classes], × [amount of munitions], × [number of classes or sessions per year]).

1.1.2. Include annual requirement for each munitions type.

1.1.3. State if requirement is an increase or decrease over previous requirements. Include the previous years' consumption reports.

1.1.4. State when munitions are required.

1.1.5. Be reviewed and validated by MUFM, who forwards the request to AFCESA/CEXD, 139 Barnes Drive, Tyndall AFB FL 32403-5319, for Air Staff coordination and inclusion in future revisions of this catalog. If the user does not have a MUFM, the supporting MAJCOM staff director will appoint one in writing that will coordinate requests through the servicing MAJCOM munitions staff before sending to AFCESA/CEXD.

1.2. Changing Authorizations. Send requests for change to the MUFM and MAJCOM munitions staff for review and validation. The request will be forwarded, with supporting documents, to AFCESA/CEXD, 139 Barnes Drive, Tyndall AFB FL 32403-5319, for coordination.

1.2.1. Units may request one-time authorizations for items needed for special projects, missions, or training not covered by this catalog.

1.2.2. Units may request interim changes to a munitions authorization.

1.2.3. Each request will explain how the new requirement was calculated.

1.3. Forecasting Requirements. Use the authorizations in this catalog to develop annual munitions forecasts. All ground security munitions (e.g., small arms ammo, grenades, simulators) are found in AFCAT 21-209V1. In some cases, ground security munitions are listed and highlighted within this catalog to provide a comprehensive "package" (i.e. course requirements, UTCs, etc). Each activity responsible for an operational mission or for providing training with munitions will:

1.3.1. Determine type and quantity of munitions needed to support peacetime and contingency needs.

1.3.2. Determine number of participants or classes requiring training during the forecast period and compute required munitions quantities.

1.3.3. Provide total munitions requirement as directed by the MUFM, in accordance with AFI 21-201, *Conventional Munitions Maintenance Management*, Chapter 14. MUFM will validate all unit and consolidated forecasts for accuracy and completeness.

1.4. Records and Reports. Records and reports of munitions expended are used to establish, validate, and fund forecast submissions. The MUFM uses these records and reports of past munitions expenditures to establish realistic forecasts in support of future operational and training requirements.

1.5. Training Requirements Validation. MUFM will review the ground munitions forecast and ensure Category D (training and planned operations; see **paragraph 1.6.3** for definitions of Category Codes) requirements are consistent with historical expenditure data. MUFM will also justify any requirement deviating from the previous year's validated requirement by more than 10 percent, and prepare justifications for increases.

1.6. Special Instructions:

1.6.1. To use or procure commercial off-the-shelf (COTS) explosives and munitions, requesting units must process the request and comply with the guidelines in AFI 21-201 and AFMAN 91-201, *Explosive Safety Standards*, paragraph 10.

1.6.2. If training conditions do not permit use of identified munitions, MAJCOMs may authorize units to forecast for substitute items (e.g., approved units may forecast for and use 7.62 mm ball in lieu of 7.62 mm tracer due to fire hazards on their training ranges).

1.6.3. Munitions requirements forecast categories include (see Agile Munitions Support Tool, for a complete listing of the major categories and requirements codes of non-nuclear munitions):

1.6.3.1. Category A: Used for shelf/service life expiration and for high use assets. Do not use to replace unserviceable assets damaged or worn out from daily use.

1.6.3.2. Category B: Ground Forces and EOD Combat Requirements: Munitions required for all ground forces for use upon arrival at deployed locations. Includes munitions deployed from a home base for mobility, unit relocation, augmentation and pre-positioned assets for incoming forces. Examples of a Category B item are all munitions on EOD UTC 3-day supply deployable packages (BB) and EOD mobility pre-positioned stocks (BE). *NOTE:* Category B munitions can be and should be used and reported under Category B when deployed in support of named operations.

1.6.3.3. Category C: Non-expendable Training and Test: Peacetime static-level (non-WRM and non-consumable) munitions. Munitions used in weapons loading, or assembly training, including dispensing systems. Includes items used for display, hands on, and familiarization training. For example, flights should use code C CC (Non-expendable inert training to include EOD, Emergency Management, CE, Live Support, etc.) for non-expendable training assets.

1.6.3.4. Category D: Peacetime consumable munitions. This category includes all items consumed and not covered by other categories, and will be used for all planned operations, range operations, and training. For example, all range operations are planned operations and fall under this category (D DR). Other examples include air shows, demonstrations, open houses, internal and external training, exercises, inspections, ammunition disposition request (ADR) operations, non-emergency (routine) support to other Federal agencies, and any other routine and or planned events).

1.6.3.5. Category E: Munitions expended for research, development, test and evaluation (RDT&E) support, and for special projects. For example, the weapons systems evaluation program (WSEP), test ranges, and support to RDT&E at other locations for tools, techniques and or weapon system development, will forecast requirements and expend munitions under this category.

1.6.3.6. Category T: Munitions expended for current/daily operations, such as airlift flights over hostile areas, drug interdiction, EOD, Security Forces and Office of Special Investigations (OSI) protection of installations, equipment, and personnel. These munitions are not intended to be, but **may** be, expended during the course of **real world/daily** operational situations; however, this category is not a substitute to meet training requirements. Some examples of use are EOD render-safe munitions stocks for render safe procedures (RSP) and emergency response operations (unplanned events); Bird Aircraft Strike Hazard (BASH), ceremonial, and animal control; and munitions required for firepower demonstrations.

1.6.3.7. Category Y: EOD disposal munitions used to process items disposed of by EOD. This category is not used to submit annual munitions forecast requirements.

1.6.3.8. Category Z: Standard Air Munitions Package (STAMP) munitions designated for pre-positioning at STAMP locations for rapid deployment. STAMP requirements are identified by AFCESA/CEX to the Global Ammunition Control Point (GACP), Air to Surface Munitions Directorate (OO-ALC/WM), and prepared for call-forward by theater commanders as needed in their area of responsibility (AOR).

1.7. Lead Time for Delivery of Munitions. New or increased munitions requirements may not be available for two or more years after the forecast. Programming, approval, funding, and procurement actions make up this lead time. The Air Force's ability to support operational and training requirements directly depends upon the timeliness and accuracy of forecasts. Munitions users should order only what they can use and use what they order.

1.8. Ground Munitions Forecasting Tool (GMAT). "HQ AFCESA/CEXD, HQ AFSFC/SFXW and the OO-ALC/GHGMB Global Ammunition Control Point are developing a web based tool to view and calculate ground and demolition munitions authorizations to improve the accuracy of fiscal year forecasting. In the event of discrepancies between the tables in this AFCAT and the tables in the web based forecasting tool, the tables in the web based forecasting tool will take precedence. The GMAT can be accessed through the AMMO & AMST - Global Ammunition Control Point (GACP) application via the Air Force Portal at **https://www.my.af.mil/ammoprod/wm/**.

Chapter 2

TRAINING, EXERCISE, COMPETITION, AND DEMONSTRATION MUNITIONS AUTHORIZATIONS

Section 2A—HQ USAF Directed Training, Exercise, and Competition Authorizations

2.1. Emergency Destruction Team (EDT) Allowances. The munitions items in Table 2.1 are authorized to provide training and to maintain proficiency of EDT members. Authorizations in Column A are per individual EDT member or instructor. Authorizations in Column B are total annual requirements per unit tasked to maintain emergency destruction capability.

Table 2.1. EDT Munitions Allowances Table.

Munitions Item	A	B
Cap, blasting, practice, non-electric, FSC 1375 M097	0 each	50 each
Cap, blasting, practice, electric, FSC 1375 M098	0 each	25 each
Fuse, blasting, time, inert, FSC 1375 M671	0 ft	100 ft
Charge, demolition, 1.25 lb, C-4, M112, FSC 1375 M023	2 each	4 each
Cap, blasting, electric, special, M6, FSC 1375 M130	3 each	200 each
Cap, blasting, non-electric, special, M7, FSC 1375 M131	3 each	100 each
Cord, detonating, PETN, FSC 1375 M456	6 ft	600 ft
Fuse, blasting, time, M700, FSC 1375 M670	12 ft	100 ft
Igniter, time blasting fuse, M60, FSC 1375 M766*	2 each	50 each

*The prime item is the M81 Igniter. The M60 (DODIC M766) igniter is suitable for time fuse but not shock tube, whereas the M81 igniter may be used for time fuse or shock tube. Units may require both items on account and should use M60 igniters to initiate time fuse until the inventory is depleted.

NOTE:

1. Authority to obtain explosives is contingent upon the base's capability to provide storage, handling, and safety instructions.

Section 2B—Security Forces (SF) Training and Competition Authorizations (OPR: AFSFC/SFO)

2.2. Explosive Detector Dog Proficiency Training Allowances. *NOTE:* For deployed explosive detector dog (UTC QFEBP) allowances, see Table 3.8.

Table 2.2. Explosive Detector Dog Proficiency Training Munitions Allowances Table.

Munitions Item	Per Dog	Note

Munitions Item	Per Dog	Note
Charge, demolition, 1.25 lb, C-4, M112, FSC 1375 M023	6 each	1, 2, 3, 5
Charge, demolition, block, TNT, 0.5 lb, FSC 1375 M031	6 each	1, 2, 3, 5
Charge, demolition, block, TNT, 1 lb, FSC 1375 M032	6 each	1, 2, 3, 5
Charge, ammonium nitrate, 75%, FSC 1375 MN85	6 each	1, 2, 3, 4, 5
Cord, detonating, PETN, FSC 1375 M456	30 ft	1, 2, 3, 5
Dynamite, ammonium nitrate, 40%, FSC 1375 M585	6 each	1, 2, 3, 4, 5
Dynamite, nitroglycerin, 40%, FSC 1375 M587	6 each	1, 2, 3, 4, 5
Dynamite, ammonium nitrate, 50%, FSC 1375 MN04	6 each	1, 2, 3, 4, 5
Dynamite, nitroglycerin, 50%, FSC 1375 MN05	6 each	1, 2, 3, 4, 5
Dynamite, ammonium nitrate, 60%, FSC 1375 MN32	6 each	1, 2, 3, 4, 5
Dynamite, nitroglycerin, 60%, FSC 1375 MN30	6 each	1, 2, 3, 4, 5
CESK, complete, FSC 1375 MN01	1 each	1, 2, 3, 4, 5
Powder, smokeless, nitrocellulose, IMR, FSC 1375 MY57	2 each	1, 2, 3, 5
Explosive, water gel, 0.5 lb, FSC 1375 MY77	6 each	1, 2, 3, 5
Charge, demolition, 0.5 lb Semtex A, FSC 1375 MN82	3 each	1, 2, 3, 5

NOTES:

1. Authority to obtain explosives is contingent upon the base's capability to provide storage, handling, and safety instructions.

2. Explosives handled extensively should be completely changed out about every 120 days (or as directed by technical orders), or whenever dogs no longer respond to the particular substance.

3. One canine explosive scent kit (CESK) per five explosive detector dogs, or fraction thereof. Dog kennels are to restock kits, as necessary, with items listed above. Units will not order new kits based only on an item or substance becoming unserviceable.

4. Kits may have 40%, 50%, or 60% dynamite, but cannot have all three percentages.

5. If the Department of Defense Identification Number (DODIC) MN01 is unavailable, request DODIC YY72, empty wooden box containers. This wooden box contains eight empty AMMO M19A1 cans, DODIC WY89. Request other individual components as applicable.

6. Authority to obtain explosives is contingent upon the base's capability to provide storage, handling, and safety instructions.

Section 2C—Civil Engineer (CE) Training Authorizations

2.3. CE Forces, Air Force Civil Engineer Support Agency (AFCESA) Designated Training Sites, Rapid Engineers Deployable Heavy Operations Repair Squadron Engineers (RED HORSE), and Prime Base Engineer Emergency Forces (Prime BEEF):

2.3.1. The allowances in Table 2.3 are to provide training and maintain proficiency for RED HORSE explosive teams. Authorizations are per class or session for RED HORSE quarry and explosive demolition and home station training. *NOTE:* All ground security munitions (e.g., small arms ammo, grenades, simulators) are found in AFCAT 21-209V1.

Table 2.3. RED HORSE Munitions Allowances Table.

Munitions Item	Quantity
Adapter, priming, M1A4, FSC 1375 M002	60 each
Charge, demolition, 1.25 lb, C-4, M112, FSC 1375 M023	50 each
Charge, demolition, block, TNT, 0.5 lb, FSC 1375 M031	50 each
Charge, demolition, block, TNT, 1 lb, FSC 1375 M032	100 each
Charge, demolition, 40 lb, ammonium, FSC 1375 M039	4 each
Cap, blasting, practice, non-electric, FSC 1375 M097	50 each
Cap, blasting, practice, electric, FSC 1375 M098	25 each
Cap, blasting, electric, special, M6, FSC 1375 M130	60 each
Cap, blasting, non-electric, special, M7, FSC 1375 M131	60 each
Charge, shaped, demolition, 15 lb, M2A4, FSC 1375 M420	5 each
Charge, shaped, demolition, 40 lb, M3A2, FSC 1375 M421	5 each
Cord, detonating, PETN, FSC 1375 M456	1000 ft
Cord, detonating, dummy, FSC 1375 M458	100 ft
Dynamite, military, M1, FSC 1375 M591	50 each
Fuse, blasting, time, M700, FSC 1375 M670	500 ft
Igniter, time blasting fuse, M81, FSC 1375 MN08*	20 each
Igniter, time blasting fuse, M60, FSC 1375 M766*	30 each
Fuse, blasting, time, inert, FSC 1375 M671	100 ft
Charge, demolition, linear, shaped, 225 gr/ft, FSC 1375 ML15	5 each
Charge, demolition, linear, shaped, 300 gr/ft, FSC 1375 ML16	5 each
Charge, demolition, linear, shaped, 400 gr/ft, FSC 1375 ML17	3 each
Charge, demolition, linear, shaped, 500 gr/ft, FSC 1375 ML18	3 each
Charge, demolition, linear, shaped, 600 gr/ft, FSC 1375 ML19	3 each
Delay, trunkline, 17 ms, 20 ft, FSC 1375, DODIC TBD	600 each
Delay, trunkline, 42 ms, 20 ft, FSC 1375, DODIC TBD	600 each

Munitions Item	Quantity
Shock tube, FSC 1375 YY34	50,000 ft
Clip, detonating cord, M1, FSC 1375 MY01	50 each
Charge, Demolition, FSC 1375, MN47	25 each
Cap Blasting, FSC 1375, MN06	10 each
Cap, Blasting – nonelectric Delay, M15 – Shock tube, FSC 1375, MN07	100 each
Grenade, Hand, Smoke, White, M18, FSC 1330, G930	64 ea
Grenade, Hand, Smoke, Red, M18, FSC 1330, G950	64 ea
Grenade, Hand, Smoke, Green M18, FSC 1330, G940	64 ea
Grenade, Hand Smoke, Violet M18, FSC 1330, G955	64 ea
Grenade, Hand Smoke, Yellow M18, FSC 1330, G945	64 ea
Mine, Claymore, M18 Series FSC 1345, K143	12 ea
Flare, Signal, FSC 1370, L312	48 ea
Flare, Trip, FSC 1370, L495	32 ea

*The prime item is the M81 Igniter. The M60 (DODIC M766) igniter is suitable for time fuse but not shock tube, whereas the M81 igniter may be used for time fuse or shock tube. Units may require both items on account and should use M60 igniters to initiate time fuse until the inventory is depleted.

NOTE:

1. Authority to obtain explosives is contingent upon the base's capability to provide storage, handling, and safety instructions.

2.3.2. EOD Technician Authorizations. The allowances in **Table 2.4** support training and maintain proficiency of EOD technicians (OPR: AFCESA/CEX). Column A is the maximum annual authorization per EOD six-person team assigned at unit level; Column B is the maximum annual authorization per Silver Flag CoBRA training site. For locations with unequal multiples of six personnel assigned, round up to the next multiple (e.g., one to six assigned, multiply by 1; seven to twelve assigned, multiply by 2). These quantities are the maximum authorized, and by no means are they required; organizations preparing forecasts should request only the quantity needed. *NOTE:* All ground security munitions (e.g., small arms ammo, grenades, simulators) are found in AFCAT 21-209V1.

Table 2.4. EOD Munitions Allowances Table.

Munitions Item	A	B
Fuse, bomb, practice, nose, M904E2, empty, FSC 1325 F919	5 each	0 each
Fuse, bomb, practice, tail, M905, empty, FSC 1325 G172	3 each	0 each
Delay element, fuse, M9, FSC 1325 G211	6 each	0 each

Munitions Item	A	B
Signal kit, personnel distress, A/P25S-5A, FSC 1370 L119	2 each	0 each
Charge, demolition, 1.25 lb, C-4, M112, FSC 1375 M023	60 each	120 each
Charge, demolition, 0.5 lb Semtex A, FSC 1375 MN82	10 each	10 each
Charge, demolition, block, TNT, 0.5 lb, FSC 1375 M031	12 each	60 each
Charge, demolition, block, TNT, 1 lb, FSC 1375 M032	10 each	120 each
Cap, blasting, practice, non-electric, FSC 1375 M097	10 each	0 each
Cap, blasting, practice, electric, FSC 1375 M098	10 each	0 each
Cap, blasting, electric, special, M6, FSC 1375 M130	60 each	400 each
Cap, blasting, non-electric, special, M7, FSC 1375 M131	100 each	2000 each
Cartridge, .50 caliber, blank, electric impulse, FSC 1385 M174	25 each	0each
Cartridge, .50 caliber, ball, FSC 1305 A555	25 each	0 each
Cartridge, 9 mm, ball NATO, FSC 1305 A363	25 each	120000 each
Cartridge, 5.56 mm, ball (M855), FSC 1305 A059	300 each	45000each
Cord, detonating, PETN, FSC 1375 M456	1000 ft	50000 ft
Dynamite, military, M1, FSC 1375 M591	30 each	0 each
Firing device, demolition, pressure type, M1A1, FSC 1375 M631	0 each	5 each
Firing device, demolition, pressure release, M5, FSC 1375 M627	0 each	5 each
Firing device, demolition, pull release, M3, FSC 1375 M629	0 each	5 each
Firing device, demolition, release, M1, FSC 1375 M631	0 each	5 each
Fuse, blasting, time, M700, FSC 1375 M670	1000 ft	5000 ft
Charge assembly demolition M183 COMP 4, FSC 1375 M757	2 each	0 each
Igniter, time blasting fuse, M81, FSC 1375 MN08 †	40 each	500 each
Igniter, time blasting fuse, M60, FSC 1375 M766 †	60 each	1000 each
Firing device, demolition, multipurpose, M142, FSC 1375 ML03	6 each	0 each
Cutter, EXROD, Mk 23, FSC 1375 ML04	3 each	0each
Cutter, EXROD, Mk 24, FSC 1375 ML05	3 each	0 each
Charge, demolition, linear, shaped, 75 gr/ft, FSC 1375 ML13*	5 each	0 each
Charge, demolition, linear, shaped, 225 gr/ft, FSC 1375 ML15	5 each	0 each

Munitions Item	A	B
Charge, demolition, linear, shaped, 400 gr/ft, FSC 1375 ML17	5 each	0 each
Charge, demolition, linear, shaped, 600 gr/ft, FSC 1375 ML19	5 each	0 each
Charge, demolition, linear, shaped, 125 gr/ft, FSC 1375 ML14	5 each	0 each
Charge, demolition, linear, shaped, 300 gr/ft, FSC 1375 ML16	5 each	0 each
Charge, demolition, linear, shaped, 500 gr/ft, FSC 1375 ML18	3 each	0 each
Det-a-sheet, 0.083 in thick, feet, FSC 1375 M980	38 ft	380 ft
Shock tube, FSC 1375 YY34	5000 ft	40000 ft
Avon L-Tech round, Mk 275, 12 ga, FSC 1305 AA63	10 each	180 each
Ultra Velocity Slug L-Tech round, Mk 274, 12 ga, FSC 1305 AA62	10 each	40 each
Popper L-Tech round, Mk 276, 12 ga, FSC 1305 AA64	10 each	30 each
Medium velocity blank, Mk 278, 12 ga, FSC 1305 AA66	10each	50 each
Cartridge, Mk 277, enhanced blank, FSC 1385 DWEC	10 each	30 each
Cartridge, Mk 279, steel slug, FSC 1385 DWED	10 each	30 each
Cartridge, Mk 280, aluminum slug, FSC 1385 DWEE	10 each	30 each
Dearmer, lightweight disposable, Mk 171, FSC 1375 YY32	6 each	30 each
Grenade, hand, incendiary, AN-M14, FSC 1330 G900	24 each	160 each
Grenade, smoke red, FSC 1330 G950 (each)	16 each	464 each
Grenade, hand Smoke Green, FSC 1330 G940	0 each	464 each
Grenade, Hand Smoke Violet, FSC 1330 G955	0 each	464 each
Simulator, Airburst, M74A1, FSC 1370, L495	2 each	0 each
Simulator, Boobytrap, M118, FSC 1370, L599	10 each	96 each
Simulator, Explosive, FSC 1370, L600	10 each	150 each
Simulator, Hand Grenade, FSC 1370, L601	10 each	1000 each
Container, Shaped Charge, FSC 1375, M475	10 each	0 each
Container, Shaped Charge, FSC 1375, M476	10 each	0 each
Container, Shaped Charge, FSC 1375, M482	20 each	0 each
Container, Shaped Charge, FSC 1375, M483	10 each	0 each
Container, Shaped Charge, FSC 1375, M484	10 each	0 each

Munitions Item	A	B
Cartridge, 7.62mm Ball Linked, M80, FSC 1305 A143	300 each	216000 each
Cartridge, 5.56mm Blank, M200, FSC 1305 A080	0 each	43,320 each
Cartridge, 7.62mm Blank, XM82, FSC 1305 A111	0 each	12,800 each
Simulator, Projectile Ground Burst M115, FSC 1370, L594	5 each	1000 each
Explosive cutting tape, 2400 gr/ft, charge demo, low hazard, flexible linear shaped Mk 145-0, FSC 1375 MM53	20 ft	40 ft
Explosive cutting tape, 5400 gr/ft, charge demo, low hazard, flexible linear shaped Mk 145-0, FSC 1375 MM54	20 ft	40 ft
Cap Blasting with 500 ft Shock Tube, FSC 1375 MN88**	10 each	500 each
Cap Blasting with 1,000 ft Shock Tube, FSC 1375 MN90**	10 each	800 each

*Indicates items that are obsolete, not currently in inventory, or not supported, but authorized for EOD unique training value. Units are reminded that ordering some items may result in a newer-generation; linked-replacement item being delivered (e.g., ordering an M1 firing device, DODIC M631, may result in receiving an M142 firing device). Some older items, once turned in, may never be available again. Units are encouraged to research items before forecasting and or taking any action.

**Items may be substituted with MN02 or MN03 assets.

NOTE:

1. Authority to obtain explosives is contingent upon the base's capability to provide storage, handling, and safety instructions.

†The prime item is the M81 Igniter. The M60 (DODIC M766) igniter is suitable for time fuse but not shock tube, whereas the M81 igniter may be used for time fuse or shock tube. Units may require both items on account and should use M60 igniters to initiate time fuse until the inventory is depleted.

2.3.3. Readiness Challenge Competition (OPR: AFCESA/CEX), including PRIME BEEF, Priority Improved Management Effort Readiness In Base Services (PRIME RIBS), EOD, disaster preparedness (readiness), public affairs, and chapel requirements. The munitions listed in Table 2.5 are authorized for subordinate command, MAJCOM, and Air Force team competition. ***NOTE:*** All ground security munitions (e.g., small arms ammo, grenades, simulators) are found in AFCAT 21-209V1. This table will only be utilized for scheduled Readiness Challenge Competitions.

Table 2.5. Readiness Challenge Competition Munitions Allowances Table.

Munitions Item	Per Team
Bomb, GP, 500 lb, empty with lug, FSC 1325 E486	20 each

Munitions Item	Per Team
Fin assembly, bomb retarder, Mk 15 Mod 4, FSC 1325 F391	20 each
Adapter-booster, bomb, tail, empty, M147, FSC 1325 F409	20 each
Adapter-booster, bomb, nose, empty, T45E7, FSC 1325 F411	20 each
Fin assembly, bomb, conical, MAU-93/B, FSC 1325 F664	20 each
Retarder fin, bomb, air inflatable, BSU-49/B, FSC 1325 GY25	20 each
Adapter, priming, M1A4, FSC 1375 M002	10 each
Charge, demolition, block, TNT, 1 lb, FSC 1375 M032	10 each
Cap, blasting, electric, special, M6, FSC 1375 M130	10 each
Cap, blasting, non-electric, special, M7, FSC 1375 M131	10 each
Cord, detonating, PETN, FSC 1375 M456	200 ft
Firing device, demolition, pressure type, M1A1, FSC 1375 M631	200 each
Firing device, demolition, pressure release, M5, FSC 1375 M627	200 each
Firing device, demolition, pull release, M3, FSC 1375 M629	200 each
Firing device, demolition, release, M1, FSC 1375 M631	200 each
Fuse, blasting, time, M700, FSC 1375 M670	150 ft
Igniter, time blasting fuse, M81, FSC 1375 MN08*	10 each
Firing device, demolition, multipurpose, M142, FSC 1375 ML03	200 each
Clip, detonating cord, M1, FSC 1375 MY01	10 each

*The prime item is the M81 Igniter. The M60 (DODIC M766) igniter is suitable for time fuse but not shock tube, whereas the M81 igniter may be used for time fuse or shock tube. Units may require both items on account and should use M60 igniters to initiate time fuse until the inventory is depleted.

NOTE:

1. Authority to obtain explosives is contingent upon the base's capability to provide storage, handling, and safety instructions.

2.3.4. Combat Battlefield Airman Training. This course prepares EOD Airmen for tactical combat in direct support of offensive and defensive operations, provides advanced weapons training, and prepares Airmen to operate in a remote field environment with emphasis on mounted and dismounted operations. It will prepare Airmen to conduct tactical level EOD operations independent of the airbase enabling plug and play capability with sister Services. *NOTE:* All ground security munitions (e.g., small arms ammo, grenades, simulators) are found in AFCAT 21-209V1.

Table 2.6. Combat Battlefield Airman Training Course.

Munitions Item	Quantity
Cartridge, 5.56 mm, ball (M855), FSC 1305 A059	240,000 each
Cartridge, 7.62 mm, NATO Special Ball, FSC 1305 A136	180,000 each
Cartridge, 9 mm, ball NATO, FSC 1305 A363	90,000 each

NOTE:

1. Authority to obtain explosives is contingent upon the base's capability to provide storage, handling, and safety instructions.

Section 2D—Air Education and Training Command (AETC) Operations Training School Authorizations

2.4. AETC Training:

2.4.1. Munitions Systems Apprentice Course, J3ABR2W031-0A0B (OPR: AETC/DOOI):

2.4.1.1. The munitions items in **Table 2.7** are authorized for conducting live explosives demonstrations in support of munitions apprentice training. Quantities listed in Column A are authorized for initial qualification training of each class or group of twenty-four students. Quantities listed in Column B are authorized for instructor qualification for each instructor assigned per year. *NOTE:* All ground security munitions (e.g., small arms ammo, grenades, simulators) are found in AFCAT 21-209V1.

Table 2.7. Live Explosives Training Munitions Allowances Table.

Munitions Item	A	B
Bomb, practice, BDU 33D/B, FSC 1325 E969	1 each	1 each
Cartridge, signal, practice bomb, AN/Mk 4 Mod 3, FSC 1325 F557	1 each	1 each
Clip, detonating cord, FSC 1375 M001	1 each	1 each
Adapter, primer, M1A4, FSC 1375 M002	1 each	1 each
Charge, demolition block, M112, FSC 1375 M023	1 each	1 each
Charge, demolition, block, TNT, 0.5 lb, FSC 1375 M031	1 each	1 each
Cap, blasting, electric, special, M6, FSC 1375 M130	3 each	3 each
Cap, blasting, non-electric, special, M7, FSC 1375 M131	4 each	3 each
Cord, detonating, PETN, FSC 1375 M456	120 ft	120 ft
Fuse, blasting, time, M700, FSC 1375 M670	20 ft	20 ft
Igniter, time blasting fuse, M60, FSC 1375 M766*	3 each	3 each

*The prime item is the M81 Igniter. The M60 (DODIC M766) igniter is suitable for time fuse but not shock tube, whereas the M81 igniter may be used for time fuse or shock tube. Units may require both items on account and should use M60 igniters to initiate time fuse until the inventory is depleted.

NOTE:

1. Authority to obtain explosives is contingent upon the base's capability to provide storage, handling, and safety instructions.

    2.4.1.2. The items listed in **Table 2.8** are authorized for bomb assembly training in the munitions apprentice course. Quantities indicated are required annually and are authorized for bench stock.

Table 2.8. Bomb Assembly Training Munitions Allowances Table.

Munitions Item	Quantity
Drive assembly, ATU-35, FSC 1325 BY29	400 each
Wire, arming, FSC 9505 BY31	20,000 ft
Ferrule, FSC 1325 EY21	200 each
Clip, arming, FZU-18, FSC 1325 EY74	150 each
Swivel and link, FSC 4030 CY72	200 each
Kit, fin retaining, FSC 1340 MY18	50 each

NOTE:

1. Authority to obtain explosives is contingent upon the base's capability to provide storage, handling, and safety instructions.

    2.4.2. EOD Preliminary Course, L3AQR3E831-000 (OPR: AETC/TTO). The items listed in **Table 2.9** are for the EOD Preliminary Course. *NOTE:* All ground security munitions (e.g., small arms ammo, grenades, simulators) are found in AFCAT 21-209V1.

Table 2.9. EOD Preliminary Course Munitions Allowances Table.

Munitions Item	Per Student	Per Class	Per Year
Cartridge, 30 mm caliber, PGU-16/A, dummy, aerojet, FSC 1305 B099	0 each	0 each	1 each
Drive assembly, ATU-35B/B, FSC 1325 BY29	0 each	0 each	1 each
Dispenser, bomb, CBU-87, FSC 1325 E851	0 each	0 each	1 each
Bomb, GP, 750 lb, M117A1E1, w/link, inert, FSC 1325 F246*	0 each	0 each	1 each
Fuse, bomb, practice, nose, M904E2, empty, FSC 1325 F919	0 each	0 each	2 each
Fuse, bomb, practice, tail, M905, empty, FSC 1325 G172	0 each	0 each	2 each

Munitions Item	Per Student	Per Class	Per Year
Warhead, 2.75 in, practice, WTU-1/B, inert, FSC 1340 H663	0 each	0 each	1 each
Rocket motor, 2.75 in, inert, FSC 1340 J103	0 each	0 each	2 each
Warhead, 2.75 in, inert, flechette, FSC 1340 JY76	0 each	0 each	1 each
Mine, antipersonnel, nonbounding, inert, XM68, FSC 1345 K139	0 each	0 each	1 each
Charge, demolition, 1.25 lb, C-4, M112, FSC 1375 M023	2 each	46 each	782 each
Cap, blasting, practice, non-electric, FSC 1375 M097	1 each	24 each	408 each
Cap, blasting, electric, special, M6, FSC 1375 M130	2each	46 each	782 each
Cap, blasting, non-electric, special, M7, FSC 1375 M131	3 each	69 each	1173 each
Fuse, blasting, time, M700, FSC 1375 M670	15 ft	350 ft	5950 ft
Fuse, blasting, time, inert, FSC 1375 M671	6 ft	96 ft	1632 ft
Igniter, time blasting fuse, M81, FSC 1375 MN08†	2 each	46 each	782 each
Cord, detonating, PETN, FSC 1375 M456	2 ft	46 ft	782 ft

*Indicates items that are obsolete, not currently in inventory, or not supported, but authorized for EOD unique training value. Units are reminded that ordering some items may result in a newer-generation, linked-replacement item being delivered (e.g., ordering an M1 firing device, DODIC M631, may result in receiving an M142 firing device). Some older items, once turned in, may never be available again. Units are encouraged to research items before forecasting and or taking any action.

NOTE:

1. Authority to obtain explosives is contingent upon the base's capability to provide storage, handling, and safety instructions.
†The prime item is the M81 Igniter. The M60 igniter (DODIC M766) is suitable for time fuse but not shock tube, whereas the M81 igniter may be used for time fuse or shock tube. Units may require both items on account and should use M60 igniters to initiate time fuse until the inventory is depleted.

2.4.3. EOD Craftsman Course, JCACP3E871 00AB. Quantities are based on twelve students per class and fifteen scheduled classes per year. These authorizations support Air Force unique EOD training conducted at Eglin AFB. Students attend this course for the award of the 7 skill level. *NOTE:* All ground security munitions (e.g., small arms ammo, grenades, simulators) are found in AFCAT 21-209V1.

Table 2.10. EOD Craftsman Course Munitions Allowances Table.

Munitions Item	Per Class	Per Year
Bomb, GP, Mk 82, FSC 1325 E485	0 ea	2 ea
Bomb, GP, 500 lb, empty with lug, FSC 1325 E486	0 ea	2 ea
Dispenser, bomb, CBU-87, FSC 1325 E851	0 ea	2 ea
Adapter-booster, bomb, nose, M148, FSC 1325 F372	0 ea	4 ea
Adapter-booster, bomb, tail, XM147, FSC 1325 F387	0 ea	4 ea
Adapter-booster, bomb, tail, M147, FSC 1325 F409	0 ea	4 ea
Adapter-booster, bomb, nose, empty, T45E7, FSC 1325 F411	0 ea	4 ea
Fuse, bomb, Mk 339, inert, FSC 1325 F817	0 ea	2 ea
Fuse, bomb, practice, nose, M904E2, empty, FSC 1325 F919	0 ea	2 ea
Fuse, dummy, FMU-72, FSC 1325 G126	0 ea	2 ea
Fuse, dummy, FMU-139(D-2), FSC 1325 G127	0 ea	2 ea
Fuse, bomb, practice, tail, M905, empty, FSC 1325 G172	0 ea	2 ea
Delay element, fuse, M9, FSC 1325 G211	0 ea	2 ea
Retarder fin, bomb, air, BSU-49/B, FSC 1325 GY25	0 ea	4 ea
Warhead, rocket, practice, inert, FSC 1340 H663	0 ea	4 ea
Rocket motor, 2.75 in, inert, FSC 1340 J103	0 ea	4 ea
Flare, dummy, aircraft, parachute, LUU-2A/B, FSC 1370 L432	0 ea	4 ea
Bomb, practice, BDU-45, FSC 1325 FO14	0 ea	4 ea
Cartridge, .50 caliber, blank, electric impulse, FSC 1385 M174	12 ea	180 ea
Charge, demolition, 1.25 lb, C-4, M112, FSC 1375 M023	30 ea	450 ea
Cap, blasting, electric, special, M6, FSC 1375 M130	24 ea	360 ea
Cap, blasting, non-electric, special, M7, FSC 1375 M131	24 ea	360 ea
Cord, detonating, PETN, FSC 1375 M456	1000 ft	15000 ft
Fuse, blasting, time, M700, FSC 1375 M670	500 ft	7500 ft
Igniter, time blasting fuse, M81, FSC 1375 MN08*	30 ea	450 ea
Igniter, time blasting fuse, M60, FSC 1375 M766*	30 ea	450 ea
Shock tube, FSC 1375 YY34	5000 ft	75000 ft
Avon L-Tech round, Mk 275, 12 ga, FSC 1305 AA63	4 ea	60 ea
Ultra Velocity Slug L-Tech round, Mk 274, 12 ga, FSC 1305 AA62	4 ea	60 ea
Popper L-Tech round, Mk 276, 12 ga, FSC 1305 AA64	4 ea	60 ea
Medium velocity blank, Mk 278, 12 ga, FSC 1305 AA66	4 ea	60 ea

Munitions Item	Per Class	Per Year
Cartridge, Mk 277, enhanced blank, FSC 1385 DWEC	4 ea	60 ea
Cartridge, Mk 279, steel slug, FSC 1385 DWED	4 ea	60 ea
Cartridge, Mk 280, aluminum slug, FSC 1385 DWEE	4 ea	60 ea
Cord, detonating, 200 gr/ft, FSC 1375 MU41 / MN33	200 ft	3000 ft
Cap Blasting with 500 ft Shock Tube, FSC 1375 MN88	4 ea	60 ea
Cap Blasting with 1,000 ft Shock Tube, FSC 1375 MN90	4 ea	60 ea
Cap Blasting with 30 ft Shock Tube, FSC 1375 YY34	4 ea	60 ea
Grenade, hand, incendiary, AN-M14, FSC 1330 G900	12 ea	180 ea

*The prime item is the M81 Igniter. The M60 (DODIC M766) igniter is suitable for time fuse but not shock tube, whereas the M81 igniter may be used for time fuse or shock tube. Units may require both items on account and should use M60 igniters to initiate time fuse until the inventory is depleted.

NOTE:

1. Authority to obtain explosives is contingent upon the base's capability to provide storage, handling, and safety instructions.

2.4.3.1. EOD Air Force Unique Course, J3ABP3E831-000. (OPR: AETC/A7COX). The items listed in **Table 2.11** are for the EOD Air Force Unique Course. Quantities are based on twelve students per class and twenty-five scheduled classes per year. These authorizations support Air Force unique EOD training conducted at Eglin AFB. Students attend this course after completion of the EOD Apprentice Course. ***NOTE:*** All ground security munitions (e.g., small arms ammo, grenades, simulators) are found in AFCAT 21-209V1.

Table 2.11. EOD Air Force Unique Course Munitions Allowances Table.

Munitions Item	Per Class	Per Year
Cartridge, .50 caliber, ball link, FSC 1305 A555	400 each	10,000 each
Bomb, practice, BDU-45, FSC 1325 FO14	1 each	25 each

2.4.4. Explosive Detector Dog Training:

Table 2.12. Explosive Detector Dog Training Munitions Allowances Table.

Munitions Item	Per Dog Entering Training	Note
Charge, demolition, 1.25 lb, C-4, M112, FSC 1375 M023	1 each	1, 2, 4
Charge, demolition, block, TNT, 0.5 lb, FSC 1375 M031	2 each	1, 2, 4
Charge, demolition, block, TNT, 1 lb, FSC 1375 M032	1 each	1, 2, 4
Charge, Demo .5LB Semtex A, FSC 1375 MN82	3 each	1, 2, 4

Munitions Item	Per Dog Entering Training	Note
Cord, detonating, PETN, FSC 1375 M456	5 ft	1, 2, 4
Dynamite, ammonium nitrate, 40%, FSC 1375 M585	2 each	1, 2, 3, 4
Dynamite, nitroglycerin, 40%, FSC 1375 M587	2 each	1, 2, 3, 4
Dynamite, ammonium nitrate, 50%, FSC 1375 MN04	2 each	1, 2, 3, 4
Dynamite, nitroglycerin, 50%, FSC 1375 MN05	2 each	1, 2, 3, 4
Dynamite, ammonium nitrate, 60%, FSC 1375 MN32	2 each	1, 2, 3, 4
Dynamite, nitroglycerin, 60%, FSC 1375 MN30	2 each	1, 2, 3, 4
Powder, smokeless, nitrocellulose, IMR, FSC 1375 MY57	1 each	1, 2, 4
Explosive, water gel, 0.5 lb tube, FSC 1375 MY77	2 each	1, 2, 4

NOTES:

1. Authority to obtain explosives is contingent upon the base's capability to provide storage, handling, and safety instructions.

2. Explosives handled extensively should be completely changed out about every 120 days (or as directed by technical orders), or whenever dogs no longer respond to the particular substance.

3. Kits can have either 40%, 50%, or 60% dynamite, but cannot have all three percentages.

4. If DODIC MN01 is unavailable, request DODIC YY72, empty wooden box containers. This wooden box contains eight empty AMMO M19A1 cans, DODIC WY89. Request other individual components as applicable.

5. Authority to obtain explosives is contingent upon the base's capability to provide storage, handling, and safety instructions.

Section 2E—Air Mobility Command (AMC) Authorizations

2.5. EOD USAF Expeditionary Center. EOD GCR forces assigned to 421 GCR Squadron EOD, AMWC (OPR: AMC/CEX), Air Force Training Management System (AFTMS) Course #AMCPREOD, are authorized the allowances listed in Table 2.13. There are fifteen students per class and seven classes are scheduled per year. These authorizations support specialty training conducted at the AMWC, and are in addition to those listed for EOD technicians elsewhere in this catalog. *NOTE:* All ground security munitions (e.g., small arms ammo, grenades, simulators) are found in AFCAT 21-209V1.

Table 2.13. EOD USAF Expeditionary Center Training Munitions Allowances Table.

Munitions Item	Annually	Per Class
Cartridge, .50 caliber, ball link, FSC 1305 A555	1050 each	0 each

Munitions Item	Annually	Per Class
Cartridge, .50 caliber, ball, API Mk 211 Mod O, RAUFOSS, FSC 1305 A606	1050 each	0 each
Cartridge, 5.56 mm, blank, FSC 1305 A080	78,480 each	0 each
Cartridge, 5.56 mm, ball (M855), FSC 1305 A059	2260 each	0 each
Cartridge, 12 ga shotgun, 7-1/2 shot, FSC 1305 A014	14 each	0 each
Cartridge, 12 ga shotgun, 00 buckshot, FSC 1305 A011	14 each	0 each
Cartridge, 9 mm, ball NATO, FSC 1305 A363	0 each	5 each
Cartridge, 7.62 mm, BA, FSC 1305 A136	2260 each	0 each
Drive assembly, bomb, ATU 35, FSC 1325 BY29	1 each	0 each
Bomb, GP, 500 lb, Mk 82, empty w/lug, FSC 1325 E486	6 each	0 each
Flex shaft, MAU 86, FSC 1325 F493	3 each	0 each
Coupler, MAU 87, FSC 1325 EY91	3 each	0 each
Dispenser, bomb, CBU-87, FSC 1325 E851	1 each	0 each
Adapter-booster, bomb, tail, empty, M147, FSC 1325 F409	6 each	0 each
Adapter-booster, bomb, nose, empty, T45E7, FSC 1325 F411	6 each	0 each
Drive shaft FZ, F/arming assembly, MAU 86B-5, FSC 1325 F493	3 each	0 each
Fuse, bomb, practice, nose, M904E2, empty, FSC 1325 F919	6 each	0 each
Fuse, bomb, practice, tail, M905, empty, FSC 1325 G172	6 each	0 each
Extension, bomb fuse, M1, inert, FSC 1325 G377**	1 each	0 each
Warhead, rocket, 2.75 in, inert, FSC 1340 H663	6 each	0 each
Rocket motor, Mk 1, inert, FSC 1340 J103	6 each	0 each
Simulator, artillery, M80, FSC 1370 L378	7 each	0 each
Simulator, hand grenade M116A1, FSC 1370 L601	50 each	0 each
Cord, detonating, dummy, FSC 1375 M458	150 ft	0 ft
Cap, blasting, practice, electric, FSC 1375 M098	25 each	0 each
Grenade, incendiary, AN-M14, FSC 1330 G900	0 each	16 each
Grenade, hand smoke, green, M18, FSC 1330 G940	0 each	23 each
Grenade, hand smoke, red, M18, FSC 1330 G950	0 each	6 each
Grenade, hand smoke, violet, M18, FSC 1330 G955	0 each	6 each
Grenade, hand smoke, yellow, M18, FSC 1330 G945	0 each	6 each
Charge, demolition, 1.25 lb, C-4, M112, FSC 1375 M023	0 each	60 each
Charge, demolition, block, TNT, 0.5 lb, FSC 1375 M031	0 each	10 each
Cap, blasting, electric, special, M6, FSC 1375 M130	0 each	50 each
Cap, blasting, non-electric, special, M7, FSC 1375 M131	0 each	60 each
Cartridge, .50 caliber, blank, electric impulse, FSC 1385 M174	0 each	10 each
Coupling, base firing device, FSC 1375 M327	0 each	25 each
Charge, shaped, demolition, 15 lb, M2A3, FSC 1375 M420	0 each	1 each
Cord, detonating, PETN, FSC 1375 M456	0 ft	600 ft
Dynamite, military, M1, FSC 1375 M591	0 each	15 each
Firing device, demolition, pressure release, M5, FSC 1375 M627	0 each	5 each
Firing device, demolition, pull release, M3, FSC 1375 M629**	0 each	5 each
Firing device, demolition, pressure release, M1, FSC 1375 M631**	0 each	5 each

Munitions Item	Annually	Per Class
Fuse, blasting, time, M700, FSC 1375 M670	0 ft	300 ft
Igniter, time blasting fuse, M81, FSC 1375 MN08 †	0 each	25 each
Igniter, time blasting fuse, M60, FSC 1375 M766 †	0 each	25 each
Cap, blasting, practice, non-electric, FSC 1375 M097	0 each	25 each
Electric delay detonators, 15 ms, FSC 1375 M095**	0 each	3 each
Electric delay detonators, 10 ms, FSC 1375 M129**	0 each	3 each
Firing device, demolition, multipurpose, M142, FSC 1375 ML03	0 each	5 each
Cutter, EXROD, Mk 23, FSC 1375 ML04	0 each	2 each
Cutter, EXROD, Mk 24, FSC 1375 ML05	0 each	2 each
Charge, demolition, linear, shaped, 125 gr/ft, FSC 1375 ML14	0 each	1 each
Charge, demolition, linear, shaped, 75 gr/ft, FSC 1375 ML13**	0 each	1 each
Charge, demolition, linear, shaped, 225 gr/ft, FSC 1375 ML15	0 each	1 each
Charge, demolition, linear, shaped, 300 gr/ft, FSC 1375 ML16	0 each	1 each
Charge, demolition, linear, shaped, 500 gr/ft, FSC 1375 ML18	0 each	1 each
Charge, demolition, linear, shaped, 20 gr/ft, FSC 1375 ML09**	0 each	1 each
Charge, demolition, linear shaped, 60 gr/ft, FSC 1375 ML12**	0 each	1 each
Charge, demolition, linear, shaped, 600 gr/ft, FSC 1375 ML19	0 each	1 each
Pyrotechnic lead initiator, Mk 23, FSC 1375 MM93	0 each	3 each
Pyrotechnic lead initiator, Mk 24, FSC 1375 MM91	0 each	3 each
Handheld dual firing device, Mk 54 Mod 0, FSC 1375 MN14**	0 each	3 each
Non-electric detonator, Mk 121 Mod 0, FSC 1375 MM58**	0 each	3 each
Non-electric detonator, Mk 122 Mod 0, FSC 1375 MM59**	0 each	3 each
Non-electric detonator, Mk 126 Mod 0, FSC 1375 MM57**	0 each	3 each
Non-electric detonator, Mk 120 Mod 0, FSC 1375 MM55 (1000 ft)**	0 each	3 each
Explosive, water gel, FSC 1375 MY77	0 each	1 each
Det-a-sheet, 0.43 in thick, feet, FSC 1375 M980	0 each	38 feet
Cartridge, 105 mm, HE, M1, FSC 1315 C445	0 each	16 each
Cartridge, 60 mm, HE, M49, FSC 1310 B632	0 each	6 each
Cartridge, 81 mm, HE, M374, PD, M524A5 E7, FSC 1315 C256	0 each	16 each
Shaped charge, Mk 45, FSC 1375 M020	0 each	2 each
Dearmer, lightweight disposable, Mk 171, FSC 1375 YY32	0 each	2 each
Propellant powder, #7 reloader, FSC 1376 ML66	0 each	2 each
Shock tube, FSC 1375 YY34	0 ft	600 ft
Avon L-Tech round, Mk 275, 12 ga, FSC 1305 AA63	0 each	5 each
Ultra Velocity Slug L-Tech round, Mk 274, 12 ga, FSC 1305 AA62	0 each	5 each
Popper L-Tech round, Mk 276, 12 ga, FSC 1305 AA64	0 each	5 each
Medium velocity blank, MK 278, 12 ga, FSC 1305 AA66	0 each	5 each
Cartridge, Mk 277, enhanced blank, FSC 1385 DWEC	0 each	5 each
Cartridge, Mk 279, steel slug, FSC 1385 DWED	0 each	5 each
Cartridge, Mk 280, aluminum slug, FSC 1385 DWEE	0 each	5 each
Cord, detonating, 200 gr/ft, FSC 1375 MU41 / MN33	0 ft	10 ft

Munitions Item	Annually	Per Class
Charge, demolition, MK 88, FSC 1375 M997	12 each	0 each
Charge, demolition, 0.5 lb Semtex A, FSC 1375 MN82	0 each	12 each

**Indicates items that are obsolete, not currently in inventory, or not supported, but authorized for EOD unique training value. Units are reminded that ordering some items may result in a newer-generation, linked-replacement item being delivered (e.g., ordering an M1 firing device, DODIC M631, may result in receiving an M142 firing device). Some older items, once turned in, may never be available again. Units are encouraged to research items before forecasting and or taking any action.

NOTE:

1. Authority to obtain explosives is contingent upon the base's capability to provide storage, handling, and safety instructions.

†The prime item is the M81 Igniter. The M60 igniter (DODIC M766) is suitable for time fuse but not shock tube, whereas the M81 igniter may be used for time fuse or shock tube. Units may require both items on account and should use M60 igniters to initiate time fuse until the inventory is depleted.

Section 2F—Air Force Special Operations Command (AFSOC) Authorizations

2.6. Special Training:

2.6.1. Special Tactics Unit (STU) Exercises and Specialty Training (OPR: 720 OSS/MSL):

Table 2.14. STU Munitions Allowances Table.

Munitions Item	Quantity Per Year	Note
Marker, location, marine, red, Mk 25, FSC 1370 L554	100 each	4
	500 each	2
	700 each	3
	225 each	4, 5
Firing device, demolition, multipurpose, M142, FSC 1375 ML03	10 each	1
	50 each	2
	60 each	3
	40 each	4, 5
Adapter, priming, FSC 1375 M002	100 each	1
	500 each	2
	400 each	3
	225 each	4, 5

Munitions Item	Quantity Per Year	Note
Charge, demolition, 1.25 lb, C-4, M112, FSC 1375 M022	600 each	2
	2000 each	3
	480 each	4, 5
	0 each	1
Charge, demolition, block, TNT, 1 lb, FSC 1375 M032	225 each	2, 4, 5
	750 each	3
	100 each	1
Cap, blasting, non-electric, special, M7, FSC 1375 M131	1125 each	2, 4, 5
	3000 each	3
	4 each	1
Shaped charge, demolition, 15 lb, composition B, FSC 1375 M420	20 each	2
	50 each	3
	24 each	4, 5
	3000 each	1
Cord, detonating, PETN, FSC 1375 M456	15,000 ft	2
	12,000 ft	3
	13,500 ft	4, 5
	5 ft	1
Firing device, demolition, M1A1, pressure, FSC 1375 M631	25 each	2
	20 each	3, 4, 5
	5 each	1
Firing device, demolition, M5, pressure release, FSC 1375 M627	25 each	2
	20 each	3, 4, 5
	5 each	1
Firing device, demolition, M3 or M1, pull release, FSC 1375 M629 or M631.	25 each	2
	20 each	3, 4, 5
	4,000 each	1
Fuse, blasting, time, M700, FSC 1375 M670	20,000 ft	2
	16,000 ft	3, 4, 5
	300 ft	1
Igniter, time blasting fuse, M60, FSC 1375 M766*	1500 each	2
	2000 each	3

Munitions Item	Quantity Per Year	Note
	1200 each	4, 5
	0 each	1
Squib, electric, flash vented, M1, FSC 1377 M842	90 each	2, 4, 5
	300 each	3
	0 each	1
Cartridge, delay, CCU-89/A, FSC 1377 MH88	50 each	2
	100 each	3
	25 each	4, 5
Cap, blasting, practice, electric, FSC 1375 M098	25 each	1, 2, 3, 4, 5
Cord, detonating, dummy, FSC 1375 M458	100 ft	1, 2, 3, 4, 5
Cap, blasting, practice, non-electric, FSC 1375 M097	50 each	1, 2, 3, 4, 5
Fuse, blasting, inert, FSC 1375 M767	100 ft	1, 2, 3, 4, 5

*The prime item is the M81 Igniter. The M60 (DODIC M766) igniter is suitable for time fuse but not shock tube, whereas the M81 igniter may be used for time fuse or shock tube. Units may require both items on account and should use M60 igniters to initiate time fuse until the inventory is depleted.

NOTES:

1. 720 Special Tactics Group (STG)

2. 21, 22, and 23 Special Tactics Squadron (STS), 123 Special Tactics Flight (STF).

3. 24 STS.

4. 321 STS.

5. 320 STS.

6. Authority to obtain explosives is contingent upon the base's capability to provide storage, handling, and safety instructions.

   2.6.2. Combat Control Unit (CCU) Training (OPR: 720 OSS/MSL). *NOTE:* All ground security munitions (e.g., small arms ammo, grenades, simulators) are found in AFCAT 21-209V1.

Table 2.15. CCU Munitions Allowances Table.

Munitions Item	Per Person	Per CCU
Adapter, priming, FSC 1375 M002	5 each	0 each
Charge, demolition, 1.25 lb, C-4, M112, FSC 1375 M023	24 each	0 each
Charge, demolition, block, TNT, 1 lb, FSC 1375 M032	5 each	0 each
Cap, blasting, non-electric, special, M7, FSC 1375 M131	25 each	0 each
Cartridge, delay, 20-second, M252, FSC 1377 M308	0 each	50 each
Charge, demolition, shaped, 15 lb, composition B, FSC 1375 M420	0 each	24 each
Cord, detonating, PETN, FSC 1375 M456	240 ft	0 ft
Firing device, demolition, M1A1, pressure, FSC 1375 M631	0 each	10 each
Firing device, demolition, M5, pressure release, FSC 1375 M627	0 each	10 each
Firing device, demolition, M3, pull release, FSC 1375 M629	0 each	10 each
Fuse, blasting, time, M700, FSC 1375 M670	240 ft	0 ft
Igniter, time blasting fuse, M60, FSC 1375 M766*	25 each	0 each
Clip, cord, detonator, FSC 1375 MY01	10 each	0 each
Cap, blasting, practice, electric, FSC 1375 M098	0 each	25 each
Cord, detonating, dummy, FSC 1375 M458	0	100 ft
Cap, blasting, practice, non-electric, FSC 1375 M097	0 each	50 each
Fuse, blasting, inert, FSC 1375 M767	0	100 ft

*The prime item is the M81 Igniter. The M60 (DODIC M766) igniter is suitable for time fuse but not shock tube, whereas the M81 igniter may be used for time fuse or shock tube. Units may require both items on account and should use M60 igniters to initiate time fuse until the inventory is depleted.

NOTE:

1. Authority to obtain explosives is contingent upon the base's capability to provide storage, handling, and safety instructions.

2.6.3. Air Force Special Operations School Course on "Dynamics of International Terrorism" (OPR: USAFSOS/SOED-I). *NOTE:* All ground security munitions (e.g., small arms ammo, grenades, simulators) are found in AFCAT 21-209V1.

Table 2.16. "Dynamics of International Terrorism" Course Munitions Allowances Table.

Munitions Item	Annually
Charge, demolition, 1.25 lb, C-4, M112, FSC 1375 M023	15 each
Cap, blasting, electric, special, M6, FSC 1375 M130	300 each
Cord, detonating, PETN, FSC 1375 M456	1000 ft

Munitions Item	Annually
Dynamite, military, M1, FSC 1375 M591	15 each
Charge, Demo, 0.5lb SEMTEX A, FSC 1375 MN82	30 each

NOTE:

1. Authority to obtain explosives is contingent upon the base's capability to provide storage, handling, and safety instructions.

Section 2G—United States Special Operations Command (USSOCOM) Central and United States Central Command (USCENTCOM) Authorizations

2.7. Combat Control Apprentice Course, L3ABP1C231-000 (OPR: AETC/DOOI). *NOTE:* All ground security munitions (e.g., small arms ammo, grenades, simulators) are found in AFCAT 21-209V1.

Table 2.17. Combat Control Apprentice Course Munitions Allowances Table.

Munitions Item	Quantity
Fuse, blasting, time, M700, FSC 1375 M670	1500 ft
Cord, detonating, PETN, FSC 1375 M456	4000 ft
Cap, blasting, practice, non-electric, FSC 1375 M097	120 each
Cord, detonating, dummy, FSC 1375 M458	400 ft
Fuse, blasting, time, inert, FSC 1375 M671	400 ft
Igniter, time blasting fuse, M60, FSC 1375 M766*	270 each
Charge, demolition, 1.25 lb, C-4, M112, FSC 1375 M023	400 each
Charge, shape, M2A4, 15 lb, CP8, FSC 1375 M420	5 each
Charge, demolition, block, TNT, 1 lb, FSC 1375 M032	300 each
Adapter, priming, FSC 1375 M002	100 each
Cap, blasting, non-electric, special, M7, FSC 1375 M131	300 each
Cap, blasting, electric, special, M6, FSC 1375 M130	70 each
Cap, blasting, practice, electric, FSC 1375 M098	25 each
Cord, detonating, dummy, FSC 1375 M458	100 ft
Cap, blasting, practice, non-electric, FSC 1375 M097	50 each
Fuse, blasting, inert, FSC 1375 M767	100 ft

*The prime item is the M81 Igniter. The M60 (DODIC M766) igniter is suitable for time fuse but not shock tube, whereas the M81 igniter may be used for time fuse or shock tube. Units may require both items on account and should use M60 igniters to initiate time fuse until the inventory is depleted.

NOTE:

1. Authority to obtain explosives is contingent upon the base's capability to provide storage, handling, and safety instructions.

Section 2H—United States Air Force Reserve

2.8. Expeditionary Combat Support Training & Certification Center Course. Expeditionary Combat Support training and certification for the Total Force Sufficient to prepare students to participate in Silver Flag exercises, deployment, skill level upgrade or completion of Operational Readiness Inspections. This course prepares individual EOD Airmen with hands-on proficiency or refresher, contingency, and war skills training. Allowances for this course are listed in Table 2.18. *NOTE:* All ground security munitions (e.g., small arms ammo, grenades, simulators) are found in AFCAT 21-209V1.

Table 2.18. Expeditionary Combat Support Training & Certification Center Course.

Munitions Item	Per Person	Per Year
Adapter-booster, bomb, nose, empty, T45E7, FSC 1325 F411	0 ea	4 ea
Adapter-booster, bomb, nose, M148, FSC 1325 F372	0 ea	4 ea
Adapter-booster, bomb, tail, M147, FSC 1325 F409	0 ea	4 ea
Adapter-booster, bomb, tail, XM147, FSC 1325 F387	0 ea	4 ea
Avon L-Tech round, Mk 275, 12 ga, FSC 1305 AA63	4 ea	60 ea
Bomb, GP, 500 lb, empty with lug, FSC 1325 E486	0 ea	4 ea
Bomb, GP, 750 lb, M117A1E1, w/link, inert, FSC 1325 F246*	0 ea	1 ea
Bomb, GP, Mk 82, FSC 1325 E485	0 ea	2 ea
Bomb, practice, BDU-45, FSC 1325 FO14	0 ea	4 ea
Cap Blasting with 1,000 ft Shock Tube, FSC 1375 MN90	4 ea	60 ea
Cap Blasting with 30 ft Shock Tube, FSC 1375 YY34	4 ea	60 ea
Cap Blasting with 500 ft Shock Tube, FSC 1375 MN88	4 ea	60 ea
Cap, blasting, electric, special, M6, FSC 1375 M130	60 ea	400 ea
Cap, blasting, non-electric, special, M7, FSC 1375 M131	24 ea	360 ea
Cap, blasting, practice, electric, FSC 1375 M098	10 ea	0 ea
Cap, blasting, practice, non-electric, FSC 1375 M097	24 ea	408 ea
Cartridge, .50 caliber, ball, FSC 1305 A555*	120 ea	1200 ea
Cartridge, .50 caliber, blank, electric impulse, FSC 1385 M174	12 ea	180 ea
Cartridge, 30 mm caliber, PGU-16/A, dummy, aerojet, FSC 1305 B099	0 ea	10 ea
Cartridge, 7.62mm Linked, FSC 1305 A143* (each)	300 ea	3000 ea

Munitions Item	Per Person	Per Year
Cartridge, Mk 277, enhanced blank, FSC 1385 DWEC	4 ea	60 ea
Cartridge, Mk 279, steel slug, FSC 1385 DWED	4 ea	60 ea
Cartridge, Mk 280, aluminum slug, FSC 1385 DWEE	4 ea	60 ea
Charge assembly demolition M183 COMP 4, FSC 1375 M757*	2 ea	0 ea
Charge, demolition, 0.5 lb Semtex A, FSC 1375 MN82	10 ea	10 ea
Charge, demolition, 1.25 lb, C-4, M112, FSC 1375 M023	30 ea	450 ea
Charge, demolition, block, TNT, 0.5 lb, FSC 1375 M031	12 ea	60 ea
Charge, demolition, linear, shaped, 75 gr/ft, FSC 1375 ML13*	3 ea	50 ea
Cord, detonating, 200 gr/ft, FSC 1375 MU41 / MN33	500 ft	5000 ft
Cord, detonating, PETN, FSC 1375 M456	500 ft	50000 ft
Cutter, EXROD, Mk 23, FSC 1375 ML04	3 ea	30 ea
Cutter, EXROD, Mk 24, FSC 1375 ML05	3 ea	30 ea
Delay element, fuse, M9, FSC 1325 G211	0 ea	2 ea
Dispenser, bomb, CBU-87, FSC 1325 E851	0 ea	2 ea
Drive assembly, ATU-35B/B, FSC 1325 BY29	0 ea	2 ea
Dynamite, military, M1, FSC 1375 M591	0 ea	30 ea
Firing device, demolition, multipurpose, M142, FSC 1375 ML03	0 ea	30 ea
Firing device, demolition, pressure release, M5, FSC 1375 M627*	0 ea	30 ea
Firing device, demolition, pressure type, M1A1, FSC 1375 M631*	0 ea	30 ea
Firing device, demolition, pull release, M3, FSC 1375 M629*	0 ea	30 ea
Firing device, demolition, release, M1, FSC 1375 M631*	0 ea	30 ea
Flare, dummy, aircraft, parachute, LUU-2A/B, FSC 1370 L432	0 ea	4 ea
Fuse, blasting, time, inert, FSC 1375 M671	50 ft	500 ft
Fuse, blasting, time, M700, FSC 1375 M670	50 ft	1000 ft
Fuze, bomb, Mk 339, inert, FSC 1325 F817	0 ea	2 ea
Fuze, bomb, practice, nose, M904E2, empty, FSC 1325 F919	2 ea	20 ea
Fuze, bomb, practice, tail, M905, empty, FSC 1325 G172	1 ea	5 ea
Fuze, dummy, FMU-139(D-2), FSC 1325 G127	0 ea	2 ea
Fuze, dummy, FMU-72, FSC 1325 G126	0 ea	2 ea
Grenade, hand, incendiary, AN-M14, FSC 1330 G900*	12 ea	180 ea
Igniter, time blasting fuse, M60, FSC 1375 M766 †	25 ea	1000 ea
Igniter, time blasting fuse, M81, FSC 1375 MN08 †	30 ea	500 ea
Medium velocity blank, Mk 278, 12 ga, FSC 1305 AA66	4 ea	60 ea

Munitions Item	Per Person	Per Year
Mine, antipersonnel, nonbounding, inert, XM68, FSC 1345 K139	0 ea	1 each
Popper L-Tech round, Mk 276, 12 ga, FSC 1305 AA64	4 ea	60 ea
Retarder fin, bomb, air, BSU-49/B, FSC 1325 GY25	0 ea	4 ea
Rocket motor, 2.75 in, inert, FSC 1340 J103	0 ea	20 ea
Shock tube, FSC 1375 YY34	5000 ft	75000 ft
Ultra Velocity Slug L-Tech round, Mk 274, 12 ga, FSC 1305 AA62	4 ea	60 ea
Warhead, 2.75 in, inert, flechette, FSC 1340 JY76	0 ea	5 each
Warhead, 2.75 in, practice, WTU-1/B, inert, FSC 1340 H663	0 ea	10 each

NOTE:

1. Authority to obtain explosives is contingent upon the base's capability to provide storage, handling, and safety instructions.

Chapter 3

OPERATIONAL MUNITIONS AUTHORIZATIONS

Section 3A—General Information

3.1. Authorization Limits. Munitions authorized in Chapter 3 are for operational peacetime, wartime, and contingency missions. They are the maximum authorizations; MUFM's should consider factors such as storage requirements when preparing munitions forecasts.

Section 3B—CE Munitions Authorizations (OPR: AFCESA/CEX)

3.2. PRIME BEEF:

    3.2.1. RED HORSE Echelon Deployments. *NOTE:* All ground security munitions (e.g., small arms ammo, grenades, simulators) are found in AFCAT 21-209V1.

Table 3.1. RED HORSE Deployment Munitions Allowances Table.

Munitions Item	Per Squadron
Grenade, smoke red, FSC 1330 G950	16 each
Adapter, primer, FSC 1375 M002	200 each
Charge, demolition, 1.25 lb, C-4, M112, FSC 1375 M023	210 each
Charge, demolition, block, TNT, 0.5 lb, FSC 1375 M031	288 each
Charge, demolition, block, TNT, 1 lb, FSC 1375 M032	240 each
Charge, demolition, block, 40 lb, cratering w/well, FSC 1375 M039	75 each
Cap, blasting, electric, special, M6, FSC 1375 M130	200 each
Cap, blasting, non-electric, special, M7, FSC 1375 M131	200 each
Charge, shaped, 15 lb, composition B, FSC 1375 M420	6 each
Charge, shaped, 40 lb, composition B, FSC 1375 M421	75 each
Cord, detonating, PETN, FSC 1375 M456	21,000 ft
Dynamite, military, M1, FSC 1375 M591	100 each
Fuse, blasting, time, M700, FSC 1375 M670	1000 ft
Igniter, time blasting fuse, M81, FSC 1375 MN08*	100 each
Charge, demolition, linear, shaped, 225 gr/ft, FSC 1375 ML15	40 each
Charge, demolition, linear, shaped, 300 gr/ft, FSC 1375 ML16	40 each
Charge, demolition, linear, shaped, 400 gr/ft, FSC 1375 ML17	36 each
Charge, demolition, linear, shaped, 500 gr/ft, FSC 1375 ML18	36 each
Charge, demolition, linear, shaped, 600 gr/ft, FSC 1375 ML19	36 each
Delay, trunkline, 17 ms, 20 ft, FSC 1375, DODIC TBD	300 each

Munitions Item	Per Squadron
Delay, trunkline, 42 ms, 20 ft, FSC 1375, DODIC TBD	300 each
Shock tube, FSC 1375 YY34	15,000 ft
Charge, Demolition, FSC 1375, MN47	150 ea
Cap Blasting, FSC 1375, MN06	70 ea
Cap, Blasting – nonelectric Delay, M15 – Shock tube, FSC 1375, MN07	90 ea
Grenade, Hand, Smoke, White, M18, FSC 1330, G930	128 ea
Grenade, Hand, Smoke, Red, M18, FSC 1330, G950	128 ea
Grenade, Hand, Smoke, Green M18, FSC 1330, G940	128 ea
Grenade, Hand Smoke, Violet M18, FSC 1330, G955	128 ea
Grenade, Hand Smoke, Yellow M18, FSC 1330, G945	128 ea
Mine, Claymore, M18 Series FSC 1345, K143	36 ea
Flare, Signal, FSC 1370, L312	96 ea
Flare, Trip, FSC 1370, L495	64 ea

*Prime item: May be substituted with M2/M60 igniters.

NOTE:

1. Authority to obtain explosives is contingent upon the base's capability to provide storage, handling, and safety instructions.

3.2.2. EOD Munitions Authorizations (AFCESA/CEX):

3.2.2.1. Mobility and WRM Munitions Authorizations. The munitions in **Table 3.2** are authorized for mobility support, WRM, and contingency operations. The munitions in column A are basic quantities (BQ) to support EOD wartime three-day supply, per assigned UTC 4F9X1. Those in column B are BQ for UTC 4F9X3. Those in column C are authorizations for prepositioned WRM, sustaining quantities at high-threat main operating bases (MOB) and contingency operating bases (COB); current prepositioned WRM multipliers are 10 times quantities listed for USAFE, PACAF and AFCENT 30 Day stocks. Quantities in column C are generally ten times the three-day supply, with some exceptions. Quantities in Column D are basic amounts to support the AFSOC unique UTC (4F9P4 and 4F9J4). Quantities in column E are for airborne EOD (UTC 4F9RJ and 4F9RC). *NOTE:* All ground security munitions (e.g., small arms ammo, grenades, simulators) are found in AFCAT 21-209V1.

Table 3.2. Mobility and WRM Munitions Allowances Table.

Munitions Item	A	B	C	D	E
Cartridge, 12 ga, shotgun, 00 buckshot, FSC 1305 A011 (each)	0	25	250	25	0

Munitions Item	A	B	C	D	E
Cartridge, 12 ga, shotgun, 7 1/2 shot, FSC 1305 A014 (each)	0	25	250	0	0
Cartridge, 7.62 Ball 4-1 Linked, FSC 1305, A131each)	0	240	0	460	0
Cartridge, .50 caliber, ball, FSC 1305 A555 (each)	0	200	0	100	0
Cartridge, 5.56 mm, ball (M855), FSC 1305 A059 (each)	0	0	0	0	500
Cartridge, 5.56 mm 4 ball/1 tracer, FSC 1305 A064 (each)	0	0	0	0	672
Cartridge, .50 caliber, API M-8, FSC 1305 A576 (each)	0	200	2000	0	0
Cartridge, .50 caliber, RAUFOSS, FSC 1305 A606 (each)	240	0	2400	0	0
Cartridge, 9 mm, ball NATO, FSC 1305 A363 (each)	0	0	0	50	270
40 mm, HEDP, FSC 1310 B546 or B568 (each)	0	0	0	0	36
Grenade, hand, incendiary, AN-M14, FSC 1330 G900 (each)	16	0	160	16	0
Grenade, smoke red, FSC 1330 G950 (each)	16	0	160	16	0
Charge, demolition, 1.25 lb, C-4, M112, FSC 1375 M023 (each)	120	0	1200	60	120
Charge, demolition, block, TNT, 1 lb, FSC 1375, M032	0	0	0	40	0
Cap, blasting, electric, special, M6, FSC 1375 M130 (each)	90	0	900	90	0
Cap, blasting, non-electric, special, M7, FSC 1375 M131 (each)	100	0	1000	100	200
Cartridge, .50 caliber, electric, FSC 1385 M174 (each)	24	48	600	72	0
Charge, shaped, demolition, 15 lb, M2A4, FSC 1375 M420 (each)	0	0	42	0	0
Charge, shaped, demolition, 40 lb, M3A2, FSC 1375 M421 (each)	0	0	40	0	0
Cord, detonating, PETN, FSC 1375 M456 (feet)	2000	0	20,000	2000	1000
Fuse, blasting, time, M700, FSC 1375 M670 (feet)	1000	0	10,000	1000	2000

Munitions Item	A	B	C	D	E
Igniter, time blasting fuse, M81, FSC 1375 MN08 † (each)	100	0	1000	100	200
Squib, electric, M1, flash-vent, FSC 1377 M842 (each)	0	0	50	0	0
Cutter, EXROD, Mk 23, FSC 1375 ML04 (each)	0	0	120	0	0
Cutter, EXROD, Mk 24, FSC 1375 ML05 (each)	0	0	100	0	0
Charge, demolition, linear, shaped, 30 gr/ft, FSC 1375 ML10 (each)	0	0	30	0	0
Charge, demolition, linear, shaped, 40 gr/ft, FSC 1375 ML11 (each)	0	0	30	0	0
Charge, demolition, linear, shaped, 75 gr/ft, FSC 1375 ML13 (each)	0	0	40	0	0
Charge, demolition, linear, shaped, 125 gr/ft, FSC 1375 ML14 (each)	0	0	50	0	0
Charge, demolition, linear, shaped, 225 gr/ft, FSC 1375 ML15 (each)	0	0	50	0	0
Charge, demolition, linear, shaped, 300 gr/ft, FSC 1375 ML16 (each)	0	0	50	0	0
Charge, demolition, linear, shaped, 400 gr/ft, FSC 1375 ML17 (each)	0	0	30	0	0
Charge, demolition, linear, shaped, 500 gr/ft, FSC 1375 ML18 (each)	0	0	30	0	0
Charge, demolition, linear, shaped, 600 gr/ft, FSC 1375 ML19 (each)	0	0	30	0	0
Det-a-sheet, 0.43 in thick, FSC 1375 M980 (feet)	76	0	760	0	0
Shock tube, FSC 1375 YY34 (feet)	5000	0	50,000	5000	0
Avon L-Tech round, Mk 275, 12 ga, FSC 1305 AA63 (each)	10	0	200	10	0
Ultra Velocity Slug L-Tech round, Mk 274, 12 ga, FSC 1305 AA62 (each)	10	0	200	0	0
Popper L-Tech round, Mk 276, 12 ga, FSC 1305 AA64 (each)	10	0	200	10	0
Medium velocity blank, MK 278, 12 ga, FSC 1305 AA66 (each)	10	0	250	10	0

Munitions Item	A	B	C	D	E
Cartridge, Mk 277, enhanced blank, FSC 1385 DWEC	25	0	200	25	0
Cartridge, Mk 279, steel slug, FSC 1385 DWED	10	0	200	10	0
Cartridge, Mk 280, aluminum slug, FSC 1385 DWEE	10	0	200	10	0
Dearmer, lightweight disposable, Mk 171, FSC 1375 YY32 (each)	0	0	100	0	0
Cord, detonating, 200 gr/ft, FSC 1375 MU41 / MN33 (feet)	0	0	400	0	0
Propellant powder, #7 reloader, FSC 1376 ML66 (each)	0	0	4	0	0
Charge, demolition, Mk 88, FSC 1375 M997 (each)	0	0	100	0	0
Cap Blasting with 500 ft Shock Tube, FSC 1375 MN88	0	0	150	100	0
Cap Blasting with 1,000 ft Shock Tube, FSC 1375 MN90	0	0	150	100	0
Container, Shaped Charge, FSC 1375, M475	0	10	0	0	0
Container, Shaped Charge, FSC 1375, M476	0	10	0	0	0
Container, Shaped Charge, FSC 1375, M482	0	20	0	0	0
Container, Shaped Charge, FSC 1375, M483	0	10	0	0	0
Container, Shaped Charge, FSC 1375, M484	0	10	0	0	0

†The prime item is the M81 Igniter. The M60 igniter (DODIC M766) is suitable for time fuse but not shock tube, whereas the M81 igniter may be used for time fuse or shock tube. Units may require both items on account and should use M60 igniters to initiate time fuse until the inventory is depleted.

NOTE:

1. Authority to obtain explosives is contingent upon the base's capability to provide storage, handling, and safety instructions.

3.2.3. Emergency RSP and Disposal Munitions. The munitions in **Table 3.3** are authorized for base support for emergency response RSP and or emergency disposal. The munitions are coded TK to support EOD emergency operations, and are equivalent to a wartime three-day supply. This list represents a minimum capability for each EOD flight to keep available and ready for immediate emergency use only. An additional allocation of these munitions will be forecasted and managed by each MAJCOM for emergencies within the MAJCOM. All munitions listed will be forecast, issued, expended, and resupplied under Category Code T.

These munitions will not be used for planned operations as described in **paragraph 1.6.4**. *NOTE:* All ground security munitions (e.g., small arms ammo, grenades, simulators) are found in AFCAT 21-209V1.

Table 3.3. RSP and Disposal Munitions Allowances Table.

Munitions Item	Quantity
Cartridge, 12 ga, shotgun, 00 buckshot, FSC 1305 A011*	25 each
Cartridge, 12 ga, shotgun, 7-1/2 shot, FSC 1305 A014*	25 each
Cartridge, 9 mm, ball NATO, FSC 1305 A363*	50 each
Grenade, hand, incendiary, AN-M14, FSC 1330 G900*	16 each
Grenade, smoke red, FSC 1330 G950*	16 each
Charge, demolition, 1.25 lb, C-4, M112, FSC 1375 M023	120 each
Cap, blasting, electric, special, M6, FSC 1375 M130	90 each
Cap, blasting, non-electric, special, M7, FSC 1375 M131	100 each
Cartridge, .50 caliber, electric, FSC 1385 M174	60 each
Cord, detonating, PETN, FSC 1375 M456	2000 ft
Fuse, blasting, time, M700, FSC 1375 M670	1000 ft
Igniter, time blasting fuse, M81, FSC 1375 MN08*	100 each
Cutter, EXROD, Mk 23, FSC 1375 ML04	12 each
Cutter, EXROD, Mk 24, FSC 1375 ML05	10 each
Charge, demolition, linear, shaped, 125 gr/ft, FSC 1375 ML14	5 each
Charge, demolition, linear, shaped, 225 gr/ft, FSC 1375 ML15	5 each
Charge, demolition, linear, shaped, 300 gr/ft, FSC 1375 ML16	10 each
Charge, demolition, linear, shaped, 400 gr/ft, FSC 1375 ML17	3 each
Charge, demolition, linear, shaped, 500 gr/ft, FSC 1375 ML18	3 each
Det-a-sheet, 0.43 in thick, feet, FSC 1375 M980	38 feet
Shock tube, FSC 1375 YY34	5000 ft
Avon L-Tech round, Mk 275, 12 ga, FSC 1305 AA63	20 each
Ultra Velocity Slug L-Tech round, Mk 274, 12 ga, FSC 1305 AA62	20 each
Popper L-Tech round, Mk 276, 12 ga, FSC 1305 AA64	20 each
Medium velocity blank, MK 278, 12 ga, FSC 1305 AA66	20 each
Cartridge, Mk 277, enhanced blank, FSC 1385 DWEC	20 each
Cartridge, Mk 279, steel slug, FSC 1385 DWED	20 each
Cartridge, Mk 280, aluminum slug, FSC 1385 DWEE	20 each

Munitions Item	Quantity
Dearmer, lightweight disposable, Mk 171, FSC 1375 YY32	10 each
Cord, detonating, 200 gr/ft, FSC 1375 MU41 / MN33	400 ft
Propellant powder, #7 reloader, FSC 1376 ML66	2 each
Charge, demolition, Mk 88, FSC 1375 M997	10 each

*Prime item: May be substituted with M2/M60 igniters.

NOTE:

1. Authority to obtain explosives is contingent upon the base's capability to provide storage, handling, and safety instructions.

3.2.4. Standard Air Munitions Packages (STAMP) (OPR: AFCESA/CEX). Two (2) EOD STAMP packages have been configured to provide rapid swing stock capability for theater commanders. AFCESA/CEX validates STAMP requirements to OO-ALC/WMR. Theater commanders coordinate with the GACP to source tasking locations for Operations Plan Time Phased Force and Deployment Data (OPLAN TPFDD). During execution, actual commitment of STAMP to commanders will be in accordance with priorities established by the Joint Chiefs of Staff (JCS).

Table 3.4. EOD STAMP Munitions Allowances Table (x 2).

Munitions Item	Quantity
Charge, demolition, 1.25 lb, C-4, M112, FSC 1375 M023	20,000 each
Cap, blasting, electric, special, M6, FSC 1375 M130	1000 each
Cap, blasting non-electric, special, M7, FSC 1375 M131	2000 each
Cord, detonating, PETN, FSC 1375 M456	10,000 ft
Fuze, blasting, time, M700, FSC 1375 M670	20,000 ft
Igniter, time blasting fuze, M81, FSC 1375 MN08*	2000 each

*Prime item: May be substituted with M2/M60 igniters.

NOTE:

1. Authority to obtain explosives is contingent upon the base's capability to provide storage, handling, and safety instructions.

3.2.5. EOD Range Clearance Operations. Table 3.5 is to be used for Range/Munitions Clearance Operations. Column A is for Small Range bases. Column B is for Large Range Bases (Hill, Nellis, Luke, Eglin, and Eielson).

Table 3.5. EOD Range Clearance Operations.

Munitions Item	A	B

Munitions Item	A	B
Charge, demolition, 1.25 lb, C-4, M112, FSC 1375 M023	3000 each	15,000 each
Fuse, blasting, time, M700, FSC 1375 M670	10,000 ft	161,000 ft
Charge assembly demolition M183 COMP 4, FSC 1375 M757	40 each	96 each
Cap, blasting, electric, special, M6, FSC 1375 M130	300 each	1,000 each
Cap, blasting, non-electric, special, M7, FSC 1375 M131	2000 each	21,000 each
Cord, detonating, PETN, FSC 1375 M456	6,000 ft	20,000 ft
Explosive cutting tape, 5400 gr/ft, charge demo, low hazard, flexible linear shaped Mk 145-0, FSC 1375 MM54	300 ft	5,000 ft
Igniter, time blasting fuse, M60, FSC 1375 M766	500 each	3000 each
Grenade, hand, incendiary, AN-M14, FSC 1330 G900 (each)	16 each	96 each

NOTE:

1. Authority to obtain explosives is contingent upon the base's capability to provide storage, handling, and safety instructions.

Section 3C—AFSOC Munitions Authorizations

3.3. Protection of Air Force Resources and Personnel (OPR: 720 OSS/MSL). All quantities authorized are per each UTC tasking, except quantities listed for 24 STS are total annual authorizations. *NOTE:* All ground security munitions (e.g., small arms ammo, grenades, simulators) are found in AFCAT 21-209V1.

Table 3.6. AFSOC UTC Munitions Allowances Table.

Munitions Item	81CTT	81RBD	81SBD	24 STS
Firing device, demo, multipurpose, M142, FSC 1375 ML03	8 each	10 each	8 each	60 each
Adapter, priming, FSC 1375 M002	90 each	50 each	50 each	400 each
Charge, demolition, 1.25 lb, C-4, M112, FSC 1375 M023	30 each	90 each	30 each	240 each
Cap, blasting, non-electric, special, M7, FSC 1375 M131	100 each	100 each	100 each	400 each
Charge, demolition, shaped, 15 lb, composition B, FSC 1375 M420	3 each	5 each	3 each	12 each
Cord, detonating, PETN, FSC 1375 M456	3000 ft	3000 ft	3000 ft	12,000 ft
Fuse, blasting, time, M700, FSC 1375 M670	600 ft	600 ft	600 ft	16,000 ft

Munitions Item	81CTT	81RBD	81SBD	24 STS
Igniter, time blasting fuse, M81, FSC 1375 MN08*	100 each	100 each	100 each	1200 each

*Prime item: May be substituted with M2/M60 igniters.

NOTE:

1. Authority to obtain explosives is contingent upon the base's capability to provide storage, handling, and safety instructions.

Section 3D—Air Force Research Laboratory (AFRL) Authorizations

3.4. AFRL Tyndall AFB Operations (OPR: AFMC/A7OX). The quantities listed in Table 3.7 are total annual authorizations under Category E.

Table 3.7. AFRL Munitions Allowances Table.

Munitions Item	Quantity
Charge, demolition, 1.25 lb, C-4, M112, FSC 1375 M023	6000 each
Charge, demolition, block, TNT, 1 lb, FSC 1375 M032	1000 each
Cap, blasting, electric, special, M6, FSC 1375 M130	96 each
Cap, blasting, non-electric, special, M7, FSC 1375 M131	120 each
Bomb, GP, 500 lb, Mk 82, HE, FSC 1325 E485	6 each
Bomb, GP, 1000 lb, Mk 83, HE, FSC 1325 E509	6 each
Cartridge, 81 mm, HE, M374, PD, M524A5 E7, FSC 1315 C256	6 each
Shock tube, FSC 1375 YY34	5000 ft
Cord, detonating, PETN, FSC 1375 M456	2000 ft
Cartridge, 12 ga, Mk 276 Popper L-Tech, FSC 1305 AA64	16 each
Cartridge, .50 caliber, electric, FSC 1385 M174	36 each
Cartridge, 7.62mm AP, FSC 1305 AA03	100 each
Propellant powder, FSC 1375 ML66	5 each
Squib Electric S75. FSC 1377, M856	120 each
Cartridge 5.56mm BALL M855 Clipped ,FSC 1305 A059	480 each
Cartridge, 9 mm, ball NATO, FSC 1305 A363	250 each
Charge, Demolition, FSC 1375, M981	76 each
Fuse, blasting, time, M700, FSC 1375 M670	500 ft
Igniter, time blasting fuse, M81, FSC 1375 MN08*	25 each
Det-a-sheet, 0.83 in thick, feet, FSC 1375 M980	76 feet
Charge assembly demolition M183 COMP 4, FSC 1375 M757	19 each
Cartridge, .50 caliber, ball, FSC 1305 A555	50 each

Munitions Item	Quantity
Cartridge, 5.56MM, Ball, FSC 1305 A071)	100 each
Cartridge, 7.62MM, Ball, FSC 1305 A130 (or sub AA11)	1680 each

NOTE:

1. Authority to obtain explosives is contingent upon the base's capability to provide storage, handling, and safety instructions.

Section 3E—SF Deployment Munitions Allowances Table

3.5. SF. The munitions in Table 3.8 are authorized for mobility support and contingency operations.

Table 3.8. UTC QFEBP Explosive Detector Dog Munitions Allowances Table.

Munitions Item	Quantity	Deployed Location
Charge, demolition, 1.25 lb, C-4, M112, FSC 1375 M023	3 each	All
Charge, demolition, block, TNT, 0.5 lb, FSC 1375 M031	6 each	All
Cord, detonating, PETN, FSC 1375 M456	30 ft	All
Charge, demolition, 0.5 lb Semtex A, FSC 1375 MN82	3 each	All

NOTES:

1. Explosives handled extensively should be completely changed out about every 120 days (or as directed by technical orders), or whenever dogs no longer respond to the particular substance.

2. If DODIC MN01 is unavailable, request DODIC YY72, empty wooden box containers. This wooden box contains eight empty AMMO M19A1 cans, DODIC WY89. Request other individual components as applicable.

3. Authority to obtain explosives is contingent upon the base's capability to provide storage, handling, and safety instructions.

TIMOTHY A. BYERS, Maj Gen, USAF
DCS/Installations, Logistics & Mission Support

Attachment 1

GLOSSARY OF REFERENCES AND SUPPORTING INFORMATION

References

AFPD 21-2, Munitions, 20 SEPT 2005

AFI 21-201, Conventional Munitions Maintenance Management, 11 DEC 2009

AFCAT 21-209V1, Grounds Munitions, 09 NOV 2007

AFMAN 33-363, Management of Records, 01 MAR 2008

Prescribed Forms

None.

Adopted Forms

AF Form 847, *Recommendation For Change of Publication*

Abbreviations and Acronyms

ABD—Air base defense

ABDR—Aircraft battle damage repair

ACC—Air Combat Command

ADR—Ammunition disposition request

AETC—Air Education Training Command

AFCAT—Air Force Catalog

AFCESA—Air Force Civil Engineer Support Agency

AFMC—Air Force Materiel Command

AFPD—Air Force Policy Directive

AFRL—Air Force Research Laboratory

AFSOC—Air Force Special Operations Command

AFTMS—Air Force training management system

AGOS—Air Ground Operations School

AMC—Air Mobility Command

AOR—Area of Responsibility

BASH—Bird Aircraft Strike Hazard

BQ—Basic quantities

CCU—Combat control unit

CE—Civil engineer

AFCENT—United States Air Forces Central

CESK—Canine explosive scent kit

CLSS—Combat logistics support squadron

COB—Contingency operating base

COTS—Commercial off-the-shelf

CRG—Contingency Response Group

DoD—Department of Defense

DODIC—Department of Defense Identification Code

EDT—Emergency destruction team

EOD—Explosive ordnance disposal

EXROD—Explosive remote opening device

FSC—Federal Stock Class

ft—Foot

ga—Gauge

GCR—Ground combat readiness

GP—General purpose

gr/ft—Grains per foot

HE—High explosive

HEDP—High explosive, dual purpose

IMR—Improved military rifle

JFCC—Joint firepower control course

lb—Pound

MAJCOM—Major command

Mk—Mark

MOB—Main operating base

ms—Millisecond

MUFM—Munitions user functional manager

MWD—Military working dog

NCAA—Non-nuclear consumable annual analysis

NETOPS—Nuclear emergency team operations

NSN—National stock number

OO—ALC/WMR—Ogden Air Logistics Center, Air to Surface Munitions Directorate, Readiness Division

OPLAN TPFDD—Operations Plan Time Phased Force and Deployment Data

PACAF—Pacific Air Forces

PAN—Percussion-actuated nonelectric

PETN—Pentaerythrite tetranitrate

PRIME BEEF—Prime Base Engineer Emergency Force

PRIME RIBS—Priority Improved Management Effort Readiness In Base Services

QUP—Quantity per Unit Pack

RDT&E—Research, development, test and evaluation

RED HORSE—Rapid Engineers Deployable Heavy Operations Repair Squadron Engineers

RSP—Render safe procedure

SEMTEX—RDX (Cyclonite), PETN (Penaerythrite Tetranitrate), and a styrene-butadiene rubber binder

SF—Security Forces

STAMP—Standard Air Munitions Package

STF—Special tactics flight

STG—Special tactics group

STS—Special tactics squadron

STU—Special tactics unit

TACC—Tactical air command and control

TNT—Trinitrotoluene

USAFE—United States Air Forces in Europe

USCENTCOM—United States Central Command

USSOCOM—United States Special Operations Command

USSR—Union of Soviet Socialist Republics

UTC—Unit type code

WRM—War reserve materiel

WSEP—Weapon system evaluation program

Terms

81CTT—UTC for special tactics team combat control operations flight.

81RBD—UTC for special tactics team combat control resupply.

81SBD—UTC for special tactics team special tactics operations flight.

4F9R6—UTC for special airborne EOD team.

QFEBP—UTC for explosive detector dog.